500
Indispensable Web Sites for
men

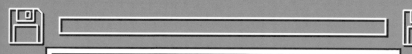

Series Editor: Colleen Collier
Revised Series Editor: Lucy Dear
Research: Jodie Geddes, Nick Daws
Additional Contributors: Sarah Wells, Jane Purcell,
Gareth Tuppenney, Jane Smith, Roya Ireland,
Christine Pountney and Richard Skinner, Ann Marangos
Page Design and Layout: Linley Clode
Cover Design: Sol Communications Ltd

Published by:
Lagoon Books
PO Box 311, KT2 5QW, UK
PO Box 990676, Boston, MA 02199, USA

www.thelagoongroup.com

ISBN: 1-902813-67-7

Printed in Thailand.

500
Indispensable Web Sites for
men

LAGOON
BOOKS

CONTENTS

INTRODUCTION

'The Internet is a tidal wave…drowning those who don't learn to swim in its waves' – Bill Gates

Over the past few years, many guides to the Internet have been written explaining how to access the Net and how to use it. But now everyone's looking for a fun and easy-to-use guide to the best sites, so here it is!

This stunning 288-page directory lists 500 essential sites for smart surfers, and is subdivided into six amazing chapters according to subject to make searching even easier!

The research has been carried out by an avid team of fun-loving Internet surfers, whose brief was to find the best sites on the web for you to enjoy – which is just what they did!

Each site is listed with the web address and several
lines of text, hinting at what you might find if you
log on and visit the web site. The book is for surfers
of all ages and abilities – you don't have to be
a computer whizz or Internet expert to use it.

Amongst the 500 fantastic web sites
listed here, you will be able to find out...

...how to make a million dollars
...where to find your missing socks
...where to purchase the very latest
in hi-tech gadgets and gizmos
...where to get hold of fake
celebrity drivers' licenses
...how to find a sponsor for your personal web page
...how to become a gambling expert
...the latest sport news, deals and scores
...where you can buy a
top-of-the-range Lamborghini

It's amazing what people put on the Internet, so here is the ultimate guide to finding all that is exciting, innovative, attainable and fantastical!

Get online for hours of fun and entertainment!

If it's new and exciting, you'll find it here!

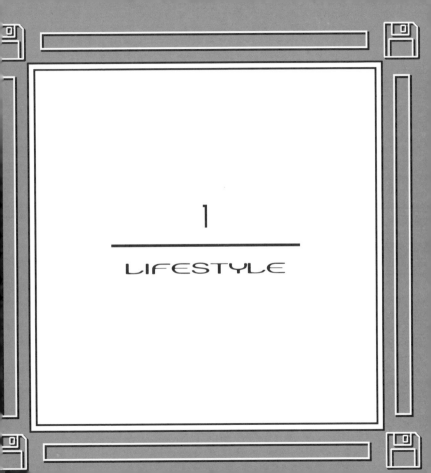

1

LIFESTYLE

Time to Quit?
http://www.quitsmokingsupport.com

It's now March, and you still haven't
followed through with that New Year's
resolution! Get all the support you need
to quit at this helpful web site.

Dating Tips
http://www.topdatingtips.com/dating-men.htm

Get the lowdown on lurve with this
great site. Check out the articles on
everything from great opening lines to
women who won't commit!

Advice for Men
http://www.askmen.com

Do women date shorter guys? How should you behave at a funeral? Just two of the many questions you'll find answered on this top advice site for men.

Good Health!
http://www.menshealth.com

This great site from *Men's Health* magazine is packed with articles and advice aimed at guys. Don't be shy guys – check it out!

Safe Sex
http://www.condomania.net

Everything you need to know about condoms and safe sex! Buy online from a huge range to make sex both safe and fun.

All About Food Labels
http://www.healthchecksystems.com/label.htm

What does fat-free really mean? How about low cholesterol? Get the answers here, but don't look just before dinner – it may put you off eating!

Cyberchicks
http://www.match.com

Maybe you are ready to consider sharing your life with someone! Too serious? Register with this site and meet people who could turn out to be good friends or maybe the love of your life.

Diet Watch
http://www.dietwatch.com

This is a web-based support group for those who haven't found losing weight very easy. Share your tips and feelings online with others in the same position.

Muscle Man
http://www.muscle-fitness.com

Stop staring at the computer screen and take some action! But first, check out the exercise regime at this site and soon you could look like Schwarzenegger.

Save Your Liver
http://alcoholism.about.com/ mbody.htm

Fed up feeling like you've crashed head on with a juggernaut? Read some sobering information at this comprehensive alcoholism info site.

Hypochondriac Heaven
http://www.intellihealth.com

Be honest! When your nose is running, do you automatically think you have flu? Does a slight headache mean your brain tumor has returned?

If you are a bit of a hypochondriac, this online medical site will give you unbiased medical advice.

Cyberdiet
http://www.cyberdiet.com

This is a well-organized site with lots of
sensible advice on following a healthy
eating plan – long-term moderation with
exercise!

Fashion Guru
http://askmen.com/fashion

Get all the hints and tips you need on
how to look trendy. There's also advice
on how to dress down and still look
good, the best hairstyles for men,
grooming, and more!

Designer Chic
http://www.home-decorating-home-decorating.com/

This massive site is packed with information on home decorating, home improvement, and interior design. Très chic!

Fit to Travel?
http://www.travelhealth.co.uk

Going abroad? This site gives detailed advice on which preparations you should make before traveling overseas, and health advice for when you reach your destination.

12

Groomed for Success
http://www.mgender.co.uk

Get advice here on looking your best,
and then order what you need from a
wide range of male grooming products.
You can even email the site's panel of
experts with your grooming queries!

Allergy Advice
http://allallergy.net

From pets to pollen, mites to mouse
droppings, whatever brings you out in
a rash you'll find links here to a huge
range of articles about it.

Drugstore Cowboy
http://www.drugstore.com

Whether you're suffering from cold and flu, or you snore like a wild hog, consult this online pharmacy for medical advice and supplies.

The Joy of Text
http://www.textually.org/

Dedicated to texting etiquette, news, information, and language. Get up to speed at this informative site!

Perchance to Dream
http://www.dreamdoctor.com

Submit your dreams to the 'Dream Doctor' and he will interpret them for you. Can't sleep? Don't worry, there are also tips for keeping insomnia at bay!

The Zoo
http://www.travelzoo.com

Think of this zoo as a protector against man-eating travel beasts, such as ridiculously high airfares! A one-stop US travel shop, this site will give you the best fares and deals.

Rough Job!
http://travel.roughguides.com

This *Rough Guide* site details over 6,000 travel destinations and gives you information, like where to find a doctor at 2.00 am in Lahore!

City Guide
http://www.cnn.com/travel

Wandering around a new city looking bewildered is a sure-fire way to get mugged! Get wise and plan ahead by downloading a city map of the place you are about to visit.

Sound Advice
http://www.thebackpacker.net

If you're going to plan each day as it comes on your overseas travels, keep some of the useful pointers featured at this site at the back of your mind.

17

Know Thy Country
http://www.newsd.com

If you want to know more about the country you are intending to visit, take a look at this site that features over 8,300 worldwide publications.

Stay with Us
http://www.travelguides.com

Wherever you want to holiday, from a small B&B to a luxury hotel, chances are you'll find your ideal accommodation in this searchable database of over 70,000 establishments worldwide.

Business Travel
**http://www.msnbc.com/
modules/travel/toolkit.asp**

It's often hard to plan a business trip
away, but at least the company has to
pay for it! Learn how to make the most of
business travel at this useful online toolkit.

Expense Account
http://www.bradmans.com

This site is just for business travelers,
providing tips on the best places to eat,
drink, and stay, in loads of destination
cities worldwide.

19

Traveling Tips
http://www.backpackers.com/

Travelers on a budget can share their experiences and provide hot tips on destinations, places to stay,and seek traveling buddies on this useful site.

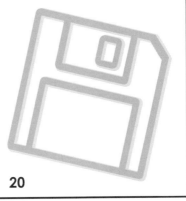

Border Control
http://www.customs.treas.gov

Have a chat to the US customs
department about the country you
are planning to visit. A good way to
determine if that bottle of whisky you
are taking over the border is legal!

Fodor's Guide
http://www.fodors.com

The *Fodor Guide* mini-books are very
useful for city travel, so check them out
at this stylish web site.

Ultimate City
http://www.ci.nyc.ny.us

Read up on the city that never sleeps,
New York, before you even leave home
at this web site, full of practical advice.

Email Me!
http://www.netcafes.com

This site contains listings of more than
4,200 Internet cafés in 140 countries to
make sure your travel news gets back
quickly to your family.

Last Minute
http://www.lastminute.com

This much-fêted site is excellent for
spontaneous trips and tickets – simply
log on for last-minute deals on flights,
packages and accommodation.

Free Flights!
http://www.frequentflier.com

The best way to fly is for free, and this
cool site explains all you need to know
about frequent-flyer points and how to
claim them.

23

Have Laptop, Will Travel
http://www.roadnews.com

Can't bear to part with your beloved laptop even on vacation? Visit here for the low-down on keeping it in tip-top condition on the road.

Real Ale
http://www.byo.com/

Learn how to brew your own ale! This site is for homebrewers everywhere, offering tips, recipes, and suggestions.

What's Cooking?
http://www.kitchenlink.com
Possibly the ultimate food site on the Web, with over 10,000 hand-selected recipes and links. Tasty!

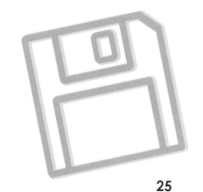

Travelers' Tips
http://www.tips4trips.com

Get the lowdown from the people who really know – your fellow travelers! As well as tips on destinations worldwide, you'll find advice here on everything from packing your luggage to traveling with children.

Juicy Jabs
http://www.tripprep.com

Consult this invaluable site to ensure you haven't forgotten to get all of those pre-travel jabs and shots. Ouch!

Cyberembassy
http://www.embpage.org

Check all your visa requirements at your local embassy online – a useful way to avoid having to stand in line for hours!

Language Net
http://www.travlang.com

An excellent site for the roving traveler to pick up a few basic phrases for use in 40 countries. Arm yourself with handy phrases such as 'Where is the railway station?'.

Railroading
http://www.trainweb.com/travel

Often the best and most peaceful way to travel around the US and Canada is by train. Check this site out for travel times and fares, and then sit back and relax as the scenery passes by.

Great Deals!
http://www.istc.org

Still young enough to be a student? Then sign up to this discount scheme site and enjoy cut-price deals to all major destinations.

Experience Oz
http://www.ozexperience.com

Experience Australia at this fantastic site that reveals the best trips 'down under'. Imagine a trip through the outback and watching sunrise over Ayers Rock!

Native Travel
http://www.vtourist.com

Paying for cabs in most major cities will have you wiring home for money before you've even reached the hotel! Check out the local transport at this site and save loads of money!

By Travelers, For Travelers
http://www.travel-library.com

This great site allows you to log on and read other people's accounts of countries you may shortly be visiting.

Go Your Own Way
http://www.etravel.org

Prefer to travel independently rather than with a tour company? Then this cool site is for you. There are articles on many popular destinations, with tips on what to take with you and how to stay safe.

Hot Stuff!
http://www.curryhouse.co.uk

A mouth-watering site for curry fans
everywhere, with recipes, authentic
cooking tips, news and reviews, and a
very useful glossary of terms.

Harbor View
http://www.viewsydney.com

This web-cam has been set up at a
location on the harbor in Sydney,
Australia. If you tire of gazing at the
Opera House, change the view!

31

Dinner Fiasco
http://www.mealsforyou.com

The dinner party that was for four has suddenly turned into a medieval banquet! Click on this brilliant dinner site and let them custom-make the recipe and cooking agenda for you!

Guinness
http://www.guinness.ie

The official Guinness web site in Ireland,
dedicated to all lovers of the dark and
frothy ale. Everything comes to he who
waits!

Oktoberfest
http://www.oktoberfest.de

Any country that dedicates an entire
month to beer, sausage and lederhosen
must have a great sense of humor.
Check out the German party animals at
this site!

33

Lonely No More
http://www.lonelyplanet.com

The guidebook publisher's site features information on many countries, plus health tips and travel-related news from around the world.

Global Gourmet
http://www.globalgourmet.com

A visual feast from all over the globe, containing excellent pointers and easy-to-follow recipes.

Simply Food
http://www.taste.co.uk

Next time ten unexpected guests turn
up for dinner, log on to this fantastic site
that is filled with hundreds of recipes,
and design and layout ideas for the
table.

Le Banquet
http://www.frenchwinesfood.com

Click on to this site for a low-down on
frogs legs, snails and fantastic wine. If
you love French food, this is the place
for you!

35

Vino Vino
http://www.winespectator.com

If you want to know what to do when the waiter asks you to taste the wine, visit this site – it's an entire ezine dedicated to wine tasting.

Cheese and Wine
http://www.cheese.com

Cheese – the perfect accompaniment to your favorite claret. You won't believe the variety mentioned at this site dedicated to the world's best cheese.

Stew Heaven!
http://funkymunky.co.za/stews.html
This site is dedicated entirely to recipes
for stews from all over the world!

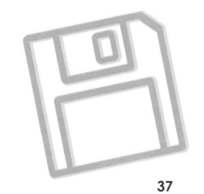

Dinner is Served
http://food.epicurious.com

An amazing site that contains thousands
of quick-and-easy recipes for every
occasion, and it also contains lots of
links to other great food sites.

Cocktail Hour
http://www.idrink.com

An excellent site to visit if you are
organizing a cocktail party. It lists over
5,000 wild, wacky, and often head-
spinning drink recipes to complement
your party atmosphere.

38

Food Channel
http://www.foodchannel.com

Feast your eyes on this web page crammed full of mouth-watering information for food lovers everywhere.

Recipes for Love
http://www.recipesource.com

Need to impress a dinner guest, but only have last night's pizza? Before you pick up the phone to order another, log onto this site and download a spectacular recipe guaranteed to impress!

Kosher
http://www.kashrusmagazine.com

If you only eat Kosher food, but are
unsure where to obtain it in a new city,
log on to this helpful site.

Why?
http://whyfiles.org

Featuring the 'science behind the news',
this web site hosts debates and features
articles on current health and news
issues to put you in the know.

Recipe Exchange
http://www.allrecipes.com/

Read other people's recipes and contribute your own at this site that positively encourages you to participate!

Fries Forever!
http://www.belgianfries.com/

If you like your fries, you'll love this site. It's all about Belgian fries, their history, recipes, and even fries' place in art and culture!

Organics
http://www.organicsdirect.co.uk

If the only food you touch is organic, you'd better log on to this natural site where you can buy fresh, organic produce online.

Carnivore
http://www.meatmatters.com

Get stuck into this juicy site, filled to the brim with meaty recipes, nutritional advice, and cute pictures of dancing sausages! Not for faint-hearted vegetarians.

Veggie Gourmet
http://www.vegweb.com

Vegetarian cooking made deliciously easy at this fun and accessible site! Your culinary expertise need no longer consist of vegetables smothered in cheese!

For Pasta Lovers
http://www.ilovepasta.org

If you thought pasta began with macaroni and ended with spaghetti bolognese the 250-plus recipes on this site will open your eyes. It's cheap, healthy and tasty as well!

Quackers
http://www.quackwatch.com

This site's aim is to 'combat health-related fraud, myths, fads, and fallacies'. If you are suffering from an illness, check this site to determine if treatments you have heard of are real or fake!

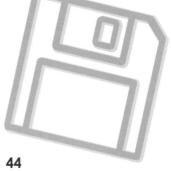

44

Know Your Rights
http://www.travel-images.com/passenger-rights-eu.html

If something goes wrong on the way to your destination, you could feel helpless. Check this site before you go to learn all about your rights as a passenger.

Go Here First
http://www.kasbah.com

Use this top guide and travel search engine to find out all you need to know about any destination from China to the Czech Republic ... before you go!

Move It!
http://www.justmove.org

You don't have to run 20 kilometers a day according to this health-conscious site – they just want you to move and provide tips and advice to get you started!

Fast Facts
http://www.refdesk.com

Need some facts at your fingertips fast? Log on to this vast reference site that aims to provide you with all the answers in a hurry.

Micro Magic Carpet
http://www.expedia.msn.com

The Microsoft travel web site, bursting with info about the places you've been dreaming of visiting, and lots of tips on how to get there.

Aloha Hawaii!
http://www.geocities.com/ TheTropics/Shores/6794

Looking for something to really impress the chicks at parties? Check it out! They'll even teach you to speak Hawaiian 'like a local' at this enchanting site!

Social Graces

http://www.debretts.co.uk/etiquette/eti quette_faq.html

If by any chance you've been invited to the Queen's for afternoon tea, and desperately need help with etiquette, this polite site has tips and advice!

Work Abroad

http://www.overseasjobs.com

Take advantage of unique opportunities by spending time working abroad. At this international employment site, you can search for the job of your dreams.

Alternative Health
**http://home.rmci.net/
michael/index4.htm**

The drugs don't work any more?
Check out alternative therapies
from acupuncture to reflexology,
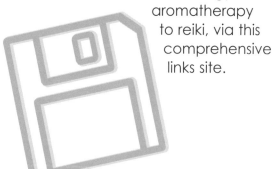
aromatherapy
to reiki, via this
comprehensive
links site.

2

MONEY, MONEY, MONEY

Who Wants to be a Millionaire?
http://abc.go.com/primetime/millionaire/millionaire_home.html

You do? Join the line; or else log on to this site that highlights the joy of previous contestants on this top-rating TV show!

Paupers Need Not Apply
http://www.vladi-private-islands.de

Once you've got a few million to spare, you can always indulge your Robinson Crusoe complex by buying yourself a private island!

Armchair Millionaire
http://www.armchairmillionaire.com

Want a head start on the road to fortune? Then log on here for tips on where to start and how to maintain long-term vision.

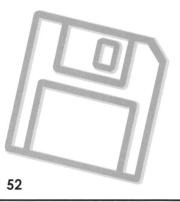

The Dollar Stretcher!
http://www.stretcher.com

Crammed full of money-saving tips,
follow the advice on this site and you'll
be a millionaire before you know it!

Splash the Cash
http://www.oanda.com

Convert any of 164 world currencies to
any other with the aid of this site. Want
to know how many Sudanese pounds
there are to an Albanian lek? This site
will tell you!

My CFO
http://www.mycfo.com

The customized services at this site will help you manage, build and preserve your wealth.

Richest Americans
http://www.forbes.com

Access 'The Forbes Four Hundred' database and find the names of all the men in Florida with a net worth of over one billion dollars – the truly choosy can search by age and marital status!

Inventions Unlimited
http://www.wybrow-innovations.co.uk/

You've got this great idea you just know will be an overnight success – but what do you do next? This web site will point you in the right direction.

Hollywood Beckons
http://www.screenwriting-on-the-net.com/

Got an idea for the next movie blockbuster? Take the free course in screenwriting on this site, then send out your script and wait for the call from Mr Spielberg.

Give Me a Price
http://ceoexpress.com

With links to major US newspapers and newsfeeds, as well as a huge database of securities and prices, this site is a must for any serious investor.

Raging Bull
http://www.ragingbull.com

Investment news and breaking headlines can be found at this site that claims to be 'leading the investor revolution'.

The Language of Money
http://www.investorwords.com

If your financial vocabulary is a bit rusty but you still want to impress your friends, this is the site to visit to find out the difference between an open-and closed-end fund.

Spamscam
http://www.junkemail.org

'Spamscam' is the official name for
email fraud – check this site on how to
report it and what Bills are being passed
to prevent it.

Bonehead Finance
http://ourworld.compuserve.com/
homepages/Bonehead_Finance

Even if you don't know your assets from
your overheads, this unstuffy site will get
you up to speed with the basics of
personal finance. And there's no ads!

58

Finance News
http://finance.uk.yahoo.com

All the latest information you need on the complete world of finance.

Make Serious Money?
http://www.rb-trading.com

Futures and derivatives need be mysteries no longer. Learn how to trade these markets for profit from Reality Based Training's 'Online Education Center', but don't risk losing your shirt!

Share Globally
http://www.global-investor.com

Have you invested around the world and are unsure how to keep track of your assets? Let 'Global Investor' keep you up-to-date with your portfolio.

What Investment?
http://whatinvestment.money.msn.co. uk/index.htm

Very useful investment tips for the private investor, including investing in property and the stock market.

Fake It!
http://hometown.aol.com/ twelfth1/page/money.htm

If you want to get rich quick, why not simply buy a fortune? These tricksters are selling phoney million dollar bills online.

You Could be a Millionaire!
http://www.moneyextra.com/faqs/milli onairefaq.html

Wouldn't it be great never to have to worry about money again? This site explores how you could make your first million.

Money Street
http://www.thestreet.com

Up-to-date news by leading reviewers
on insurance, stocks and shares.
Forums hold discussions on topics such
as 'Going back to work, is it worth
it when you've
got kids?'.

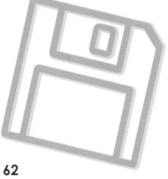

Smarty Pants
http://www.smartmoney.com/

A site for the smart and savvy money-mad amongst us! Everything you could possibly ever need to know about savings and investments.

Hanging on a Limb
http://www.familytreemaker.com

Look up your ancestors at this site that helps you trace your family tree. There may be an inheritance lying around with your name on it!

Mrs Cohen
http://www.citywire.co.uk

Mrs Cohen dishes out stock market
advice, industry news and a financial
quote of the day to give you
inspiration, at this money site.

Dollar Finder
http://www.wheresgeorge.com

This fabulous site can track any dollar
bill and let you know where it is now! All
you have to do is enter the serial
number, and the site will inform you
when and where your note has been
located!

64

Finders Keepers
http://www.foundmoney.com

If you've lost money, go to this site, type
in your personal details and they'll put a
trace on any foreign accounts that may
be in a vault waiting for you to collect it!

Buy, Buy! Sell, Sell!
http://www.quicken.com

Lots here for investors, with the latest
business news, share prices, financial
advice, and much more. A top site for
future Warren Buffets!

Microsoft
http://moneycentral.msn.com/investor

Microsoft's money page must be good – look what it did for Bill Gates!

Feeling Lucky?
http://www.gambling.com

If you're feeling lucky, why not try your hand at the various casino games and horse racing at this site? Play either for fun or for real money!

'Millionaire' Magazine
http://www.millionaire.com

If you're having trouble thinking of ways to dispose of all your hard-earned cash, read the profiles of millionaires from the last century and how they spent their millions.

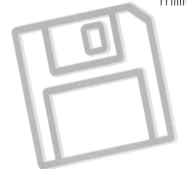

Cry 'Yahoooo'!
http://quote.yahoo.com

You'll be out on the rooftops shouting 'Yahoooo' when you discover your shares are riding high at this up-to-date site!

What Do You Get?
http://www.businessfinancemag.com

Does your salary match your true net worth? To find out, visit this online magazine's site.

Train Your Brain!
http://www.funbrain.com/cashreg/

This fun accounting game will help you to manage your finances! Maybe.

Own That Business
http://www.inc.com

Have you a business idea you're bursting to develop? Whatever the idea, before becoming your own boss you should consult this site for practical advice.

Make It Big!
http://www.stepstone.co.uk

'A change is as good as a rest', so the old saying goes! So visit this site that lists hundreds of jobs up for grabs in Europe. Brush up on your language skills first!

Share Pages
http://www.sharepages.com

Up-to-the-minute share news and rates can be found here, along with a forum for members to exchange and discuss share tips and info.

Get Paid to Surf
http://www.moo-money.com

Did you know you can get paid to surf
the web, read e-mail, use search
engines, and take part in surveys? 'Moo-
money' will help you farm these 'cash
cows'!

Make a 'Net' Profit
http://affiliate-money.com/makemoney

OK, the dotcom bubble may have burst,
but you can still make good money
from your own web site through affiliate
programs. This site will show you how.

Read All About It
http://www.randomhouse.com/ features/millionairekit

This book by Stephen L. Nelson outlines strategies and tips on saving, insurance and investment, and tells you how easy it is to earn one million bucks.

Make the Most of Your Money
http://ftyourmoney.ft.com

The *Financial Times* 'Your Money' page
aims to help readers with everything from
home buying to pensions – there's even
a free portfolio service to keep track of
your shares and other investments.

Cheapskates' Paradise
**http://www.inforesearchlab.com/
cheapskates.chtml**

A penny saved is a penny gained, as
the old proverb has it. Discover
hundreds of ways to save money here.

Don't Be Scammed!
http://www.scambusters.org

Avoid being taken in by Internet scams. Get up to speed here on the latest hoaxes, frauds, viruses, and more. Your bank manager will thank you!

News Over the Atlantic
http://www.nyse.com

Find out what's happening to shares in the city that never sleeps.

Listed List
http://www.hemscott.net

Need help tracing a company? Make this UK site, featuring a huge database of publicly quoted companies, your first stop.

Understand Finance
http://www.ibm.com/financialguide

IBM's finance page will guide you from getting started through to investors' tips – there's also a handy online glossary of terms to help you wade through the jargon.

Time for Finance
http://www.ft.com

This is a great place to visit for up-to-date business and financial news, and registration is totally free.

US Updates
http://www.amex.com

Check out movements on the Dow Jones, S&P and NASDAQ indexes.

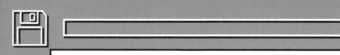

Young Investors
http://www.younginvestor.com

Here's an ultra-cool investment site for kids of all ages. Get the lowdown on investment from a child (or parent's) point of view, then drive down

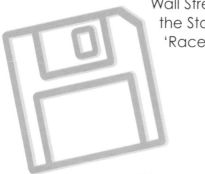

Wall Street in the Stock Car 'Race' Game!

Oz Highs and Lows
http://www.asx.com

If you've invested 'down under', this is the site to visit for share prices, info on upcoming floats, and company announcements.

Hong Kong for a Song
http://www.hkex.com.hk

The Hong Kong Stock Exchange home page, with subtitles for those who need them!

Cor Blimey
http://www.ftse.com

Whether you're looking to take out an option on a Norwegian stock, or sell a Footsie 100 company, all the pricing info you need is right here.

One Euro or Two?
http://www.euro.gov.uk

Find out all about Europe's new currency from the UK government's official web site. About the only thing it won't tell you is when – if ever – Britain will join.

World Bank
http://www.worldbank.org
Find out all about a bank dedicated to fighting poverty by raising money for development programs – their goal is a world free of poverty.

Wall Street
http://www.wsj.com
The *Wall Street Journal*'s transatlantic news site. Stay one step ahead!

Win a Million!
http://www.freelotto.com

OK, stop dreaming, and win loads of money in a flash by entering this free Internet lottery draw.

Which Bank?
http://www.aaadir.com/

With so many to choose from, this directory of banks on the Net covers the world, but is listed by continent to make searching easy.

81

In the Beginning...
http://www.ex.ac.uk/
~RDavies/arian/money.html

Find out all about the history of money
on this site – from simple bartering to
inflation and third
world debt.
Is that what they
mean by progress?

Priceless!
http://www.thefreesite.com

Visit this site for a huge range of freebies, from screen-savers to household goods. Whoever said there's no such thing as a free lunch?

Serious Money
http://www.imf.org

Get a handle on global economic issues from the International Monetary Fund's comprehensive web site. Their aim is to promote worldwide economic stability.

Need Cash?
http://www.homepagenow.com/money.html

Finding it hard to raise the money to start your own web page? Visit the site that gives you excellent advice on how to seek sponsors.

Cassandra's Revenge
http://www.cassandrasrevenge.com

Ignore the silly name – this is a friendly, down-to-earth personal finance site. It's aimed at women, but men can benefit too!

What to Do With Cash?
http://www.wgn.net/~nienhuis/

Make origami animals out of it, of course!
To find more fabulous things to do with all
those spare notes you have lying around,
get online and log on to this wacky site.

Franchise Anyone?
http://www.franchiseopportunities.com

All you need to know about owning and
operating a franchise, with thousands of
opportunities worldwide to choose from.
Select your country, and off you go!

Growing Business
http://smallbusiness.yahoo.com

If you have just started your own business and need advice on how to make it blossom, then this is the web site for you.

Foolish Advice
http://www.fool.com

Their aim is to educate, amuse and enrich you at this finance site – click on Fool's School for money advice for beginners!

Personal Advisor
http://www.thisismoney.com

A friendly online personal advisor is on hand at this site. Aimed at the average consumer rather than the practised investor, it offers practical day-to-day advice.

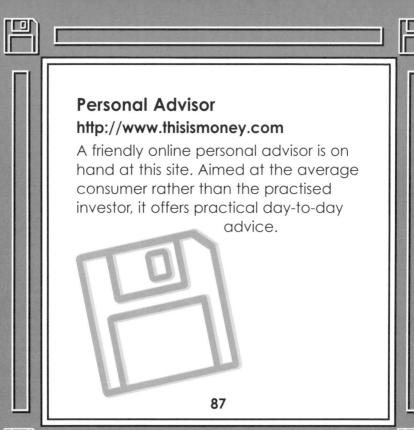

Picasso Please
http://www.artrepublic.com

Many people have made a lot of
money buying and selling art. This site is
worth having a look at to see exactly
how.

Le Chalet
http://www.french-property.com

Every le millionaire needs le holiday
home in France, non?

88

Money Mail
http://www.bankone.com

If you need to send *Money Mail* urgently to friends and family, this web site allows you to do so with the greatest of ease.

Sage Advice
http://www.wisebuy.co.uk

This online investment guide is aimed at experts and beginners alike, with unbiased information on over 100 different types of savings and investments.

Get Your Share
http://www.schwab-global.com

Charles Schwab are the world's largest
online share brokers. They offer a
low-cost execution-only service, so
don't lose your head (joke).

Work from Home
http://www.homebusinessmag.com

Lots of useful advice and information here from the web site of *Home Business Magazine*. Now, if only I can keep that cat off my keyboard...

Never Too Young
http://www.kidsmoney.org

A useful parental guide that features everything from the top ten financial principles you should impress upon your children, to tips on how kids should do paid chores.

Celeb Payouts
http://www.forbes.com/people

Which star earns $20 million per movie, and who gets paid $80,000 for a one-hour speech? See the going rates for celebs at this mag's site.

Big Boys' Toys
http://www.yachtworld.com

If money is no object, why not buy the ultimate big boy's toy at this site – a gin palace to cruise around the south of France!

92

Ex Rates
http://finance.yahoo.com

Visiting Italy shortly and need to find out how many lira there are to the dollar? It's as simple as pie with this currency converter.

Measuring Measures
http://www.french-property.com/ cgi-bin/ifp/convert.pl

Whether it's lengths, volumes, weights, or temperatures you're looking for, you can convert them all easily here at this informative site.

Hot Stock!
http://cbs.marketwatch.com

If you want the story behind the numbers, this is the web site to visit. It even boasts a hot stock tracker where you can keep track of your favorite five stocks.

Minty Fresh
http://www.usmint.gov

Take a tour of the US Mint and find out all there is to know about making money…literally!

Bake Until Golden…Rich!
http://www.geocities.com/ bourbonstreet/4968/sweetgj01.html

The proof is in the pudding! This site suggests that all it takes to make a million is the following recipe –

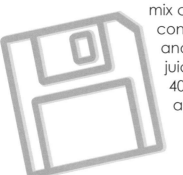

mix crackers, condensed milk and lemon juice…bake at 40 degrees and…voilà!

3

GADGETS AND GIZMOS

Naughty But Fun!
http://www.booksandgadgets.com

Feeling mischievous? Then log on to this wicked site that will point you in the direction of a fake celebrity driver's license or a remote-controlled fart machine!

Your Mission
http://www.spy.th.com/other.html

Live out your 007 fantasies at this online 'Advanced Intelligence Spy Shop' and get your hands on small wireless video cameras and disappearing ink pens.

Late Again!
http://www.excuses.co.uk

Whatever it is you've done (or haven't) this gem of a site gives you a Grade A excuse and makes you look witty too!

Cool Runnings
http://www.gizmocity.com

Imagine being able to start your car and its heater from the warmth of your breakfast table! Imagine no longer, for it is now a reality at this innovative site.

How Does It Work?
http://www.howstuffworks.com

Find out here how almost anything works, from helicopters to hypnosis, flamethrowers to fax machines. Amazing!

Virtual Babe
http://www.ananova.com

It was bound to happen – the world's first virtual newscaster! She's a cyber babe – and she can tell you the latest news too!

He's Gotta Have It
http://www.technogadgets.com

Find out about all the latest high-tech gadgets at this cool site. It's great for gift shopping – if you can resist the temptation to keep the products yourself!

Ask the Oracle
http://www.iching.com

The ancient Chinese oracle will answer all your questions. Just click your mouse over the sacred pool.

100

Gimme, Gimme, Gimme!
http://www.iwantoneofthose.com

A great online store for gadgets and gizmos 'to die for'. But can your wallet stand the strain?

Neat!
http://www.neatsite.com/gadgets.htm

A huge selection of useful things to make life easier at home, while travelling, fixing the car, or surfing the Net. Why sweat the small stuff?

101

Brainteasers
http://www.brainbashers.com

See if you can get your head around
the challenging brainteasers featured
on this site. There are also free games
you can play online, from 'Mah-Jong' to
'Hangman'!

Simon Says
http://www.mysimon.com

Need a helping hand with the shopping?
Let this online shopper lighten the load
by tracking down the best deals and the
latest gadgets so you don't have to.

Rainbow Maker
https://www.tiggypig.com/

You can stop looking as everything you ever wanted is here – a rainbow maker and a talking hairbrush to name a few!

Mobile Heaven
http://www.nokia.com

Visit the Nokia homepage. Read about all the latest models and systems, and download games such as 'Racket', 'Snake II' and 'Space Impact' to play on your handset!

Dance with Your Mouse
http://www.bustamove.com

Learn to dance online with Bustamove. You can take lessons here in salsa, hip-hop, west coast swing or east coast swing. Before you know it, you'll be a whiz on the virtual dance floor!

Global Testers Wanted!
http://www.globaltestmarket.com

Fancy trying out the latest consumer products before they hit the shops? Sign up free of charge here. You'll even be paid for giving your opinions.

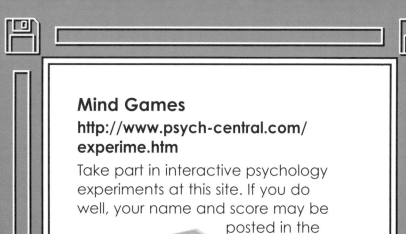

Mind Games
http://www.psych-central.com/experime.htm

Take part in interactive psychology experiments at this site. If you do well, your name and score may be posted in the 'Hall of Fame'!

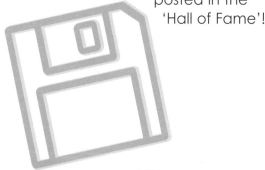

Widgets Galore
http://www.widgetchuck.com

Looking for a gadget – sorry, widget –
to liven up your web site? Here's the
place to come. There are free maps,
quotations, weather reports, news
tickers and more.

Gadgetronix
http://www.gadgetronix.com

Put your sunglasses on before you enter
this blinding site – it has all kinds of both
strange and sensible electronic goods
for your home, office and car.

MP3
http://www.wired.com/news/gizmos

If you have become addicted to the latest music technology to hit the worldwide web, then this site allows you to purchase all your MP3 needs at one place.

Can't Get Enough
http://www.sony.com

Site of one of the leading manufacturers of MP3 units – it doesn't matter how you play it, just play it loud!

Great E-Greetings!
http://www.atomflash.com/

Send free electronic greetings cards to wish someone a happy birthday, good luck or simply to say 'Hi!', from this site.

Don't Panic!
http://babelfish.altavista.com

Translate any foreign language web page into English free with Babelfish. The name comes from the universal translator fish in 'The Hitchhiker's Guide to the Galaxy' by Douglas Adams, but you don't have to stick this one in your ear!

Lights, Camera, Action
**http://www.barbizon.com/
photocat/gripgadget.html**

One for all budding photographers out
there – this site will solve all your lighting
problems and includes a huge range of
adapters, clamps, and magic arms.

Going, Going, Gone...
http://www.ebay.com

Buy or sell anything at the world's
biggest online auction house. If you're
lucky you could spot a real bargain, but
take my tip and wait till the last minute!

To Boldly Go...
http://www.startrek.com

Trekkie and proud of it? Then you'll want to make this stunning 'Star Trek' site your homepage immediately. It's packed with pictures, episode guides, news, discussion groups and far more!

No More Bets
http://www.wagerline.com

There's no risk here, as all the money is virtual – and if you do really well you might even win a prize of up to $1,000!

Pay Attention, Bond!
http://www.jamesbondmm.co.uk/q-branch.php

Check out the gadgets in every Bond film here. Want to know about the 'Acrostar Mini-jet' in Octopussy or the 'Bondola' in Moonraker? Look no further!

Make It Yourself!
http://www.invention.com

If your creative juices are flowing, have a chat to this online patent attorney. That remote-controlled lawn mower could make you a fortune!

111

Here It Is!
http://hitechdepot.com

Been online shopping all day and still can't find that special something? This web site stocks all kinds of gadgets, from Video Color Enhancers to Triple Tray DVD Players.

112

Smarten Up
http://www.smartcomputing.com

Computers still a bit of a mystery to you?
Get up to speed at *Smart Computing*
magazine's homepage. There are over
5,000 informative articles!

Home From Home
http://www.bargizmos.co.uk

With the home bar equipment and
supplies offered on this site you can now
visit the bar without ever leaving your
home!

113

Who Invented That?
http://www.enchantedlearning.com/inventors

Want to know who invented Velcro or the aerosol spray can? Find out at this must-see site for gadget junkies!

Brew It Yourself
http://www.heartshomebrew.com

If you're the type who likes to brew his own beer, this site will supply home-brewing 'goodies' such as iceless chillers, hydrometers, and mashers.

Gizmos Galore!
http://www.otherlandtoys.co.uk/

A site dedicated to fun for web-surfers of all ages! Toys, gizmos and gadgets of all kinds are available to buy online here.

Serious Fun
http://www.boysstuff.co.uk/

Everything a boy (or indeed a girl) could ever want! This site has it all - outdoor stuff, phone stuff, even naughty stuff... Enjoy!

PDA Street
http://www.pdastreet.com

PDA does not just stand for 'Public Displays of Affection' – at this site you will find the latest in computing goods and gizmos.

Etoys
http://www.etoys.com

Don't let the kids tell you what they want for Christmas – be inspired and shock the socks off them with the cool toys here, such as a 'Talking Electronic Dartboard'.

Spam
http://www.spam.com

For lovers of luncheon meat everywhere, purchase anything remotely related to 'Spam' at this site. Great buys include a pair of 'spam' flip-flops.

Stuck For a Gift?
http://www.stuckforagift.com

Can't think of a gift for that special someone? Help is at hand at this web site where gifts include 'Alien Glow-in-the-Dark Clocks'!

On the Web!
http://www.gadgetsontheweb.com

From underwater cameras to foldable compasses, this nifty site is definitely gadget heaven.

Play That Funky Music
http://www.creative.com

This site claims to 'let you plug into the power of the Internet to experience digital entertainment beyond your PC', and lets you choose the best audio products around.

Gadgets for Geeks!
http://www.thinkgeek.com/gadgets/
This cool gadget site offers 'stuff for smart masses', from security, to watches, to lights and lasers.

Gadgets for God
http://ship-of-fools.com/Gadgets/
Gadgets_body.html

Site dedicated entirely to tacky religious artefacts! From categories including food, fashion, games, and pets(?!), select the perfect tacky god-themed gift for any occasion.

Steaming!
http://www.modelrailroadandhobby.com

For the ardent train enthusiast – great-value model trains and accessories are available online from this factory-direct dealer.

Remotely Interested?
http://www.towerhobbies.com

Radio-controlled models abound at this site – from airplane kits through to race simulators. Check out the beginner's section to get started!

Weird and Wacky!
http://www.online-catalog.com
A site dedicated to everything weird
and wacky, including 'All-hazard radios'
and 'StreetPilots' so you need never ask
for directions shamefully again!

Tee-rific
http://www.golf-gadgets.com

This site easily fulfills all your golfing
needs – where else could you buy a
'Thermal Whizz GolfPack Cooler'?

My Compliments
http://complimentstothechef.com

Claiming to be a 'kitchen store and
more', this site is 'brimming with the
wonderful, incredible, amazing,
eclectic, practical...' – or so they claim
themselves!

Kitchen Gadgets
http://www.kitchen-classics.com

Use your chopping board as a mouse pad and get online to buy some cool gadgets for your kitchen, such as crème brûlée torches and electric ice shavers.

Make Life Easy
http://www.drinkinggadgets.com/

This site reviews drinking-related gadgets and rates them for their usefulness. It also provides links to web sites where you can purchase the bar-related goods. For the truly dedicated!

Being Watched!
http://www.spooktech.com

An online shopping paradise for all your surveillance needs. Log on to watch 'Busted on the Job III' – a web-cam that catches employees misbehaving!

Hot Toys
http://www.gismoworld.com

A site full of hot toys, from personal robot companions to whale-sounding mouse pads to help ease your day at the office.

On Vacation
http://www.beachcomber.com/gadget.html

If you need help carrying all your gadgets down to the beach, log on here for the ultimate in leisure time gadgetry such as a 'Beach Caddy'.

Spies Like Us
http://www.thespyshop.com

From bug detectors to electronic voice changers, it's all here at the 'Scotland Yard' Spy Shop.

Watch Out!
http://www.wonderfullywacky.com

A site guaranteed to contain the extraordinary – how about a 'Poop Mouse Candy Dispenser'? Just raise his head and stand clear of the rear!

Bonsai Potato
http://www.bonsaipotato.com

Turn a humble potato into a fabulous sacred bonsai tree! The kit includes pruning shears, tweezers, and a replica altar for your spud.

Space Age
http://www.smarthome.com

The latest in home automation and security for those dreaming of their own space-age home.

Talking Toilet Paper
http://www.talkingtp.com

A toilet roll holder that plays a message when anyone pulls the paper. Record your own message, or use one from the manufacturer's extensive library of celebrity voices!

Electronic Gadgets
http://www.gatewayelex.com/index2.htm

Do you want to keep your kids out of the refrigerator at night? Then log on here to find useful 'goodies' such as a Talking Motion Detector and a Mini CCD Camera.

Ab-zorb-ing!
http://www.zorb.com

Zorbing – rolling around in a kind of
human hamster ball – is the latest craze
for people who think bungee jumping
is for wimps! Find out more here, but
don't try it straight after a heavy meal!

Infectious Disease Underwear
**http://www.med-psych.net/doctor-
gifts/novelty-gifts.html**

A whole range of medically-themed
gifts and novelties, including
underwear patterned with images of
infectious diseases!

Life on the Edge
http://www.alt-gifts.com

This alternative gift company's web site offers big toys for big boys, and for the adventure freaks among us, they even offer life-on-the-edge experiences!

Toys 4 Guys
http://toys4guys.com

You are now entering the world of the latest funky gizmos. Feeling peckish? Visit the 'Belly Shop' for all your favorite goodies!

Thought Screen Helmet
http://www.stopabductions.com

Worried about being abducted by aliens? Help is at hand! This site takes you through how to build a useful thought screen helmet, step by step.

Pretty Potty
http://www.funkytoiletseats.com

Use these fabulous novelty toilet seats to 'Bring Your Bathroom To Life'. An exotic range of toilet seats in weird and wonderful colours and shapes – including one that opens sideways!

131

The True Blue Roo Poo Company
http://www.roopooco.com

Paperweights and jewellery made from the authentic poo of kangaroos, koala bears, and Tasmanian devils. Based in Australia, of course, but willing to ship worldwide!

Tomorrow's World
http://www.bbc.co.uk/science/tw

Based on the British TV program, this futuristic site features the latest news on science and technology, interactive online experiments, video clips from the program, and more!

132

Gadgets Galore
http://www.gadgets-galore.modifications.com

Visit this global gadget site for the latest in Playstation equipment and Internet mobile phones.

Ask the Guru
http://www.gadgetguru.com

With so many new gadgets released every week, how do you know which to buy? 'Gadget Guru' is here to help, with comprehensive buying guides on topics ranging from toys to digital cameras.

Automate Your Home
http://www.hometoys.com

Find out here how to install a computer network in your home, have multi-room audio, create your own home theater, and much more. Pretty cool!

Party Poo-per
http://www.pooppals.com

Furry pets that poop jelly beans? Mmmmm! Hand-made in the US 'by only a handful of talented ladies', but ship internationally.

134

Gadget Shop
http://www.gadgetshop.com

A range of weird and wonderful oddities, such as 'Remote Control Jammers' and 'Inflatable Audio Speakers' can be purchased online at very affordable prices.

Street Tech
http://www.streettech.com

Brush up on your tech terms with the 'Street Tech' glossary featured at this web site, and check the ratings of the latest gizmos such as 'Inverse Symbolic Calculators'.

A Christmas Robot?
http://www.robotics.com

As it says on this site, a robot makes a great gift. And here you can buy one, or learn to build your very own!

The Gizmo Page
http://www.courier-journal.com/ gizweb/index.html

This special ezine page from this online newspaper features the best in new gadgets and gizmos, such as silent instruments and the latest computers.

Tech Museum
http://store.thetech.org

Stylish technological toys for grown-ups are available at the 'Tech Museum' online store, including the 'Mini-Jupiter Kinetic Sculpture' and the 'Levitron Floating Top'.

Cool Tools
http://www.cooltool.com

This web site brings you the coolest tools on the web and hardware that goes beyond the hype.

Firebox
http://www.firebox.com/ gadgets/index.html

If remote-controlled UFOs, projection clocks and voice mail postcards are your idea of fun, check out this web site that claims that it is 'where men buy stuff'!

138

Fantasy T-Shirts
http://www.smallfaces.com

This creative t-shirt company had the neat idea of t-shirts decorated with the torso of a fantasy character and you provide the 'head'. There are over 30 great designs to choose from.

Goofy Inventions
http://www.totallyabsurd.com

Award-winning site that investigates funny inventions – there are hundreds of time-wasting treasures here, such as the 'Kissing Shield' and the 'Giant Duck Decoy'!

139

Tattooed Clothing
http://64.225.33.220/default.asp

The realistic illusion of tattoos without any of the pain or commitment! Just pull on a 'tattoo shirt' and it will look as though your arms are covered with ornate tattoos.

Opinions Wanted

http://www.epinions.com

Read other people's opinions about the latest gadgets, and post your own for the benefit of others. You'll even get paid for them!

Ask an Expert
http://www.newscientist.com/lastword

Put the experts at UK magazine *New Scientist* on the hot spot by posting your thorniest gadget questions here – and while you wait for an answer, browse through their replies to other people.

Gizmo Mania
http://www.gadgets-inc.com

Recorders, telephones, scanners, surveillance equipment, and other snooping stuff are all available here!

141

4

ENTERTAINMENT

Groovy Movies
http://www.elstreefilmtv.com

Find out about the many great movies
shot at Britain's Elstree studios – from
classic Ealing comedies to Kubrick's
'Eyes Wide Shut'.

143

Brit Flicks
http://www.filmfour.com

Remember 'Trainspotting'? Check out
the Film Four web site – a company that
produces anything but costume dramas!

Marvel-ous!
http://www.marvel.com

Visit the homepage of Marvel Comics,
home of the Incredible Hulk, Spiderman,
the X-Men, and many more. Read free
comics on the site, order Marvel
collectibles, and join the Marvel fan
club.

Miramax
http://www.miramax.com

Find out where to see the next Greenaway or Brunel films at this site dedicated to hip movies and their directors.

I'd Like to Thank...
http://www.oscars.org

Get your tuxedo out for a red-carpet visit to the site dedicated to Hollywood glamor and talent. Yes, it's the official site for Oscar.

Twentieth Century Fox
http://www.foxmovies.com

Check out the latest clips, trailers, and gossip on upcoming Hollywood blockbuster movies. Just don't expect the reviews to be entirely objective!

Books, Books, Books
http://www.amazon.com

This site has one of the world's largest selection of books for you to browse through and buy. If you fancy reviewing the latest release, you are welcome to put your thoughts online.

146

Reel Classics
http://www.reelclassics.com

A brilliant site all about the movie greats! Wallow in nostalgia – they don't make 'em like they used to!

Email a Celeb!
http://www.mailhollywood.com

Find the email address of your favorite celebrity from this site, then send for their autograph. They're all here, from Pamela Anderson to Joey Zimmerman!

Movie Bible
http://www.imdb.com

This site claims to be 'the biggest, best, most award-winning movie site on the planet'. You can check out the photos and trailers of forthcoming blockbusters, and read celeb news and interviews here.

148

Ain't It Cool?
http://www.aint-it-cool-news.com

A well-informed Hollywood insider spills all the gossip and news for you to enjoy – find out who's currently considered hot and who's not!

Movie News
http://movies.go.com

Up-to-date news and reviews mean that you won't see a turkey with the help of this site!

The Beeb
http://www.bbc.co.uk

Chat, gossip, and reviews on all your favorite British TV shows can be found at the site of one of the world's most well-renowned television channels.

Mobile Phone Games
http://www.wgamer.com

Get the lowdown on the latest and best games for your cellphone from this top review site. Where will technology take us next?

Friends Indeed
http://www.nbc.com/friends/index/html

Here's a web site dedicated to NBC's hit show 'Friends'. There's a complete episode guide, bios, and scripts – and if that's still not enough you can even download the theme tune!

Celebrity Golf
http://www.celebritygolf.com

You'd be surprised who enjoys a round of golf. Alice Cooper for example. Exclusive interviews and links to other sites featuring celebrities and golf.

151

Monster Review
http://www.mrqe.com

If you want the low-down on a film before you pay to see it, check this informative site first that contains a huge database of hundreds of films.

New Line Cinema Auction
http://www.newline.com/nlcauction/upcoming/

Newline Films regularly auction off costumes and props from their latest films – here's your chance to own Austin Powers' suit or Freddy Krueger's Leather Blade Glove.

Made Earlier
http://www.badmovies.org

Packed with some of the worst movies
ever made, this web site has great info
and plot descriptions of films such as
'Cannibal Women in the Avocado
Jungle of Death'
and 'The Brain
from Planet
Arous'!

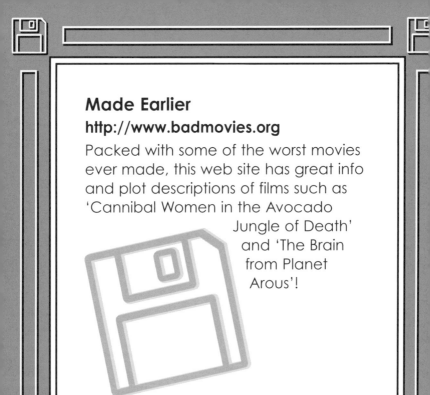

153

Blunt by Name...
http://www.bluntreview.com

All the new movie releases are reviewed on this site by critic Emily Blunt. As the name suggests, she doesn't pull any punches.

Celebrity Death Match
http://www.mtv.com/onair/deathmatch

The homepage of the television series of the same name. Come to this site to see the two Mansons or the Spice Girls battle it out in the ring.

Beatbox Betty
http://www.beatboxbetty.com

Beatbox Betty provides funky and upbeat Hollywood reviews from virtual reality land.

Xena The Warrior Milkmaid
http://www.warriormilkmaid.com

A spoof site for all fans of Xena Warrior Princess, watch Xena the milkmaid battle Cowlisto in 'Bovine Intervention' and other tales.

Oh the Humanity!
http://www.ohthehumanity.com

Check out this hilarious site for some
truly toe-curling celluloid catastrophes,
and view 'the worst films ever witnessed
by mortal eyes'. They said it!

Gamespy
http://www.gamespy.com

I spy with my little eye…a program that
is extremely useful for locating games
and servers on the Net. This site also
features a 'Hall of Fame' and the latest
reviews.

The Sims
http://thesims.ea.com

Here's the world's favorite simulation game, The Sims. Read tips and tricks on how to create your own communities, view screenshots of the game, and enter contests to win cool prizes!

Shockwave
http://www.shockwave.com

This multi-media site has an impressive array of choices – log on to games both old and new, cartoons, and greetings. This site really does have it all!

Free for All
http://www.pogo.com

Swing by this sizzling site for dozens of free games, quizzes, puzzles and more. Even the casino games are free, and there are cash prizes (paid for by advertising) for the best scores!

MP3 Search
http://www.mp3.lycos.com

Start your search for all things MP3-related here. Be warned – once you start, you won't be able to stop as there are some amazing link sites featured here too.

Get Down
http://www.cmj.com/mp3

Once you've sorted out your MP3 knowledge, it's time to start using it. This is one of the most popular MP3 portals on the Net. Log on and listen!

Raider Babe
http://www.cubeit.com/ctimes

Are you hooked on 'Tomb Raider'?
Do you admire the butt-kicking, high-
octane goddess that is Lara Croft?
There's lots of great info on this classic
game to be found here.

Cards Bonanza
http://www.zone.msn.com

This mammoth games site brings you
classic card games, such as 'Gin
Rummy' and 'Poker', as well as the best
in virtual reality 3D ones.

160

Blaster
http://www.planetunreal.com

Virtual gun-slinging matches have risen in popularity over the last five years, so let off some steam at the end of a hard day by pretending you're John Wayne!

I Wanna Be Famous
http://www.iwannabefamous.com

Making ordinary people famous one person at a time. Submit a photo and profile and get your fifteen minutes of fame.

Vampires Beware
http://www.buffyupn.com

Are you a fan of the hit TV show 'Buffy the Vampire Slayer'? Of course you are! Well, here's the official web site, with profiles of the show's stars, episode guides, video clips and much more.

Good Dog!
http://www.happypuppy.com

Get the newest free demos and shareware games from the 'Happy Puppy'. There are some tasty prizes to be won too!

New Releases
http://www.gaming-age.com

Jam-packed with all the latest game releases, it's time to get with the program and visit this site that also features news articles, charts, and previews.

163

Celebrity Diaries
http://www.diarist.net/links/
celebritydiaries.shtml

Celebrity diaries and biogs from the likes
of Anna Kournikova, William Shatner,
and Ian McKellan.

Heroes Required
http://www.blizzard.com

Blizzard Entertainment produces the
popular computer games 'WarCraft',
'Diablo' and 'StarCraft'. Visit their web
site for the latest hints, tips, cheats, and
special offers.

164

All Music
http://www.allmusic.com

Every trivia-based question on rock, pop, jazz, and blues can be found at this huge reference library of a site. Wander the corridors of music for hours.

Hobbits Welcome!
http://www.lordoftherings.net

This is the official website for Peter Jackson's blockbusting trilogy based on the epic novel by Tolkien. Come here to view stills from the movies and download some amazing trailers.

165

100 on Black
http://www.bjrnet.com

Have you always longed to learn how to play 'Blackjack'? Put your money firmly back into your pocket for the moment and get free lessons online.

Baldur's Gate
http://www.interplay.com/bgate2

Fight battles, slay monsters, cast magic spells – what more could anyone ask from a computer game? The official 'Baldur's Gate' homepage even includes screenshots and downloads!

Game Info
http://www.gamefaqs.com

Full of features and a tone of arcade games to play online, such as 'Hydro Thunder' and 'Plasma Sword', this site will keep you amused for hours.

News Just In
http://www.ign.com

With an online link to a site where you can rent games, this web site is an entertainment bonanza of sci-fi comics, new game releases, and even a movie section.

167

Myst-erious!
http://www.myst3.com

This is the homepage of 'Myst 3: Exile, a stunning adventure'. Drop by here for downloads, screenshots, background information on the game and a free newsletter.

Star Man
http://www.davidbowie.com

This is the place to find out all about rock music legend David Bowie. Weird and wonderful doesn't begin to do justice to his enigmatic web site.

Cheat Site
http://www.xcheater.com

Can't quite make it to the last level?
Let this online cheat site give you a few
pointers in the right direction.

Dungeons and Dragons
http://www.geocities.com/area51/8306

'Dungeons and Dragons' is just as
popular now as it has ever been.
Rediscover this classic game or log on
here to have a go if you missed it the
first time round.

169

Chips with Everything
http://www.chipsworld.co.uk

The console is king at Chips World. Whatever your favorite format, you'll find the best and latest games for it here. But the very best bargains are to be found among the second-hand titles!

170

How it All Began
http://www.geekcomix.com/vgh

This site is packed with fascinating information about the 'video game'. From 'Pong' to 'PlayStation', it's all here, and there's even a look at what home video gaming could offer in the future!

More Fun and Games
http://www.tombola.com

Win cash and book tokens playing free games like 'Hamster Race' at this crazy site. It's UK-based, but anyone in the world can enter!

171

Free for All Fun
http://www.uproar.com

Play games and take part in trivia quizzes, competing against other players online for cash and prizes. Be warned – you may discover that 'you're not as smart as you like to think you are'!

Make it Easy on Yourself
http://www.cheatstation.com

Whoever said cheats don't prosper? Here you'll find helpful hints and downright cheats for over 8,000 games on 40 different platforms. Phew!

DVD File
http://www.dvdfile.com/

Latest releases and sneak previews of films to come are all here. Check it out and see if you agree with the Editor's Choice.

TV Ark
http://www.tv-ark.org.uk

Superb British TV nostalgia site with a vast array of info, pictures, theme tunes, and loads more. Search by channel or by genre.

Party On!
http://www.ministryofsound.com

The cool site of one of the world's hottest dance clubs – hear all the latest mixes by their top resident DJs.

Jungle Boogie
http://www.jungle.com

Looking for an all-in-one shop that stocks your entire entertainment needs? 'Jungle' is a warehouse on the web with tons of top-brand computers, software, videos, and games.

174

Celebrities Distorted
http://www.quirked.com/distortions

Countless of celebrity photos distorted for comic effect. Includes an A-Z search to find your favourite celeb.

Music Man
http://www.peoplesound.com

If you tell the guys at this site the type of music you enjoy, they will compile a personal list of tracks for you to download and listen to!

175

MP3
http://www.mp3.com

Confused about the latest technology in music? This site explains MP3s in clear and concise terms so you won't feel ignorant and left out.

Wanna Record Contract?
http://www.vitaminic.co.uk

'Vitaminic' features music by thousands of unsigned bands in 250 different genres. If you're in a band, the site lets you distribute your music online free of charge!

Where it's at
http://www.ubl.com

You have a song going round your head, you know the band's name but don't know where to find details about them. Log on to this great site and they will give you everything you need to know, apart from their home address of course!

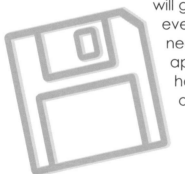

177

Time Out
http://www.timeout.com

A comprehensive online guide to gigs
and clubs featuring all types of music
worldwide can be found here at this
cool ezine site.

Rock and Roll
http://www.rollingstone.com

Get the latest buzz from the world
of music and entertainment from the
web site of America's *Rolling Stone*
magazine.

MTV
http://www.mtv.com

The most famous music television station has its own web site, featuring exclusive interviews with top artists and movie soundtrack downloads.

Crazy Chat
http://www.jerryspringer.com

With its provocative – and often downright salacious – topics, Jerry Springer's TV chat show has become an international phenomenon.

Strike a Pose
http://www.wbr.com/madonna

If the 'material girl' makes you want to strike a pose, check out her very own web site. It's packed with the latest sizzling news and gossip on the ever-changing Ms. Ciccone.

The Stones
http://www.rollingstones.com

They keep on rolling and gather no moss, so visit the baddest boys in rock and find out what they are up to at the moment – they're still misbehaving!

180

Beatlemania
http://thebeatles.com

This site features the history and a great photo library of one of the greatest bands of the 60s (some would say of all time!).

Hotel Trauma
http://www.harmony-central.com

A site written by band members – everything you need to know about performing and acting like a rock star. No TVs out of hotel windows please!

Men Who Look Like Kenny Rogers.
http://www.
menwholooklikekennyrogers.com

After a certain age, a lot of men start to look like Kenny Rogers. So many that this site has had to close to new submissions. But there's almost 1,000 photos in the picture gallery, a guide on How To Look Like Kenny, and, um, a corn muffin recipe.

Going for a Song
http://www.sheetmusicdirect.com

Experiencing songwriter's block? Then let this great site provide sheet music for you to download at those times when the harmony just won't happen!

Disco Fever
www.70disco.com

A web site entirely devoted to 1970's disco music. Profiles of bands, charts from the 70s, and more!

Bite-sized Reviews
http://www.foocha.com

A fresh new site that features 40 resident, individual and honest writers, reviewing everything in the world of entertainment. Log on for the very latest!

Video Hits and Misses
http://www.vh1.com

This music channel is now available in cyberspace and showcases artists that have now disappeared from stardom – revisit the bad hair and clothes of your youth!

184

Trivia Heaven
http://www.80s.com

Great resource for parties – simply print
off the 80s trivia questions at this site
and let the fun begin!

Best in Show
http://www.worldbeardchampionships.
com/index.html

The World Beard Championships is held
every two years. But if you think your
own beard is pretty handy and you
want to enter, you'll face stiff
competition – just check out some of
the beauties here!

All Singing, All Dancing
http://www.musicals101.com

From 'Singin' in the Rain' to 'Les Miserables', this web site is packed with news and info on the shows that have been pulling people into the theaters for years.

Turtle Art
www.turtlekiss.com

Artworks by the world's only professional turtle artist, Koopa. You can buy Koopa's original artworks or commission something brand new. Koopa doesn't care. Koopa is a turtle.

Y'all Come Now
http://www.cmt.com

Come to this site to visit the spiritual
home of Dolly Parton, the Dixie Chicks,
and Garth Brooks. If it's country, it's here!

Roadside America
**http://www.roadsideamerica.com/
vortex.html**

A guide to offbeat roadside attractions
across the United States. Jamestown,
ND has the world's largest buffalo of
course, but the controversy over who
has the world's largest chair rages on.

187

5

DREAM
MACHINES

Rolling in Class
http://www.rrab.com

Rolls Royce and Bentley are synonymous
with classy, luxurious cars. This site has
photos and a brief history of every
model ever built. Timeless classics!

Hog Heaven
http://www.harley-davidson.com

The ultimate two-wheeled machines are
shown here in all their glory! Discover
that not all Harley-Davidson riders need
a forest of facial hair – just most of them!

189

Water Laughs
http://www.formulaboats.com

We'd all spend our lottery winnings on a speedboat or three, and this site shows you just what you could spend your money on, and how fast it would go!

Wheely Sexy
http://www.fantasycars.com

Ferrari, Lamborghini, Lotus, Porsche – all names synonymous with speed, power, and desire! These machines are featured in-depth at this site, with envy-inspiring photos.

Formula 1
http://communities.msn.co.uk/f1

If speed is your thing, why not discuss the latest Grand Prix action in the MSN F1 Community? You can with this adrenaline-filled site!

Plane Crazy
http://www.fighter-planes.com

Budding Top Guns will love this look at the latest jet fighters. Great action shots and technical data can be found here, but not how much they cost!

Strip Tease
http://www.dragracingunderground.com

The ultimate fantasy cars are shown in fantastic tyre-burning action at this site. Great photos and videos give an insight into those lucky enough to be allowed behind the wheel!

Boys Toys
http://www.flightfantasy.com

Anyone with a spare $1,000,000 should check out this site for jets, helicopters and yachts that look larger and more luxurious than most homes!

192

Driven to Distraction
http://www.supercars.net

Dream machines galore can be found here, with hundreds of photos of the world's most exciting cars. Something for everyone to enjoy – technical info and plenty of shiny metal!

Concept Cars
http://www.conceptcarz.com/

With hundereds of makes and models to chose from, this is the ultimate site for speed freaks. Vroom!

Adventurer Ahoy!
http://www.adventure-plus.com/

Check out this adventure tour operator in the US that offers sea kayaking, white-water kayaking, rock climbing and mountaineering at all levels. Adrenaline levels will surely rise!

Rotor Way
http://www.helis.com

A must for whirlybird fans! Find out all about the history of helicopters on this fantastic site!

Bug Me
http://www.dune-buggy.com

Be inspired to fly over sand dunes with only a roll cage between you and the sand at this site. Speed, danger, and big tyres – who could possibly ask for more?

195

Kitted Out
http://www.kitcar.com

Kit cars are becoming faster, cheaper, and better-looking. Be inspired by the many great photos at this site, then start building the model that's right for you!

Chute Me
http://www.para-cycle.com

You too can fly through the air on a bike attached to a parachute! This amazing machine is growing in popularity, so check out this web site to view the very latest.

196

Talking Cars
http://www.carenthusiast.co.uk

You can almost smell the motor oil at this online car magazine. Motor show reports, new car road tests and motorsport features are all here, plus check out the weekly features 'All Torque' and 'Steering Column'.

Purr-fect
http://www.jaguarcars.com

Fast, sleek, shiny...and that's just the web site! Images of every Jag ever made are available here!

197

Triumph-ant!
http://www.triumph-motorcycles.ltd.uk

Find out all about the classic British bike here. As well as a showroom displaying the company's latest models, you can take a virtual tour of the Triumph factory in Leicestershire.

See for Yourself
http://www.automotive-online.com

Log on to this cool site for the latest news and information on the automotive industry. There are road tests and reviews, and even video clips of the latest models.

198

Keep on Truckin'
http://www.layover.com

Not exactly a dream machine, but a great vehicle web site nonetheless, featuring everything to do with the world of trucking!

Lotus
http://www.lotuscars.co.uk

Featuring the latest news and a detailed dealer's guide, this official Lotus web site features a production timeline and, of course, all the info on the cars themselves.

Tinker Away
http://www.autoshop-online.com

Keep your own personal dream machine on the road with in-depth advice from this non-profit-making site. Now, what did I do with that wheel spanner?

License-plate Mania
http://www.alpca.org/

Crazy about license plates? You can join license plate collectors and aficionados from all over the world by logging on to this official website!

Ferrari
http://www.ferrari.it

Italian chic and style are very much in evidence at this bilingual site of one of the ultimate dream machines – check out its history, the cars, and upcoming events.

Space Vehicles
http://www.spacefuture.com

Ever wondered how you might travel effortlessless backwards and forwards from space? Check out this site to find out!

201

Bike Net
http://www.bikenet.com

Buy anything from helmets to bikes themselves on this great site! Also features reviews of the latest products and road test advice.

Paeony F1
http://www.paeonygames.com

You don't have to have the driving skills of Ralph Schumacher to be allowed on a Formula One track – this virtual racing game lets you race safely.

Burn Rubber!
http://www.motonline.com

Superbikes are the two-wheel equivalent
of Formula 1 racing cars. This is the
official world championship web site,
and it does them proud with news,
features and some blinding photographs.

It's All Here!
http://www.moto-directory.com

Featuring complete listings of motoring
clubs and associations, a great
collector's section, and much more, this
web site is a motoring paradise.

Rally Around
http://www.scca.org

The Sports Car Club of America runs both professional and amateur rallying in the US. Their site is crammed with information about rallying and rally clubs, along with news and background on world-class rally championships.

Model Cars
http://www.ewacars.com

If you are a model car enthusiast, visit this site that has one of the largest selections of model cars on the Net.

Top Gear
http://www.topgear.com

Owners of all makes of vehicles chat online here about their cars, and it is an easy way to find out if a car will suit you. The web site of a popular British motoring TV program, it also features a whole host of road tests and opinions to get you racing.

205

Glamor and Glitz!
http://www.ytmag.com

Parts, antiques and restoration advice can be found at this site dedicated to this piece of machinery! To what am I referring? Log on to find out.

The Quad King
http://www.suzukicycles.com

Log on here for the lowdown on the Quad King from Suzuki. It's the ultimate quad bike – 'built to handle the toughest jobs' – and yours for a mere $6,000!

Aviation Antics
http://www.aso.com

If money is no object, visit the 'Aircraft Shopper Online' site and buy everything from Amphibian planes to an Executive Boeing 737 for $38,000,000!

Aprilia
http://www.aprilia.com

Claiming to be 'the site of wonder', Aprilia's official web site contains up-to-date racing history, and a complete listing of new and old models.

Hot Wheel Auction
http://www.cacars.com

This web site is an auction and marketing site for all makes and models of cars, and features great color pics to ease your fears about purchasing online.

I Want Wheels
http://www.carseverything.com

Whatever your driving requirements, you are certain to find it here. They can sell you car parts, send out appraisal forms, organize free credit, and even let you in on a few tricks of the trade.

Porsche
http://www.porsche.com

A name synonymous with glamor and speed – view all the models both old and new and, check out upcoming events.

For the Love of Cars...
http://www.bumpstop.com

Loads of crazy customised automobiles are pictured on this wacky site, along with forums and events where you can meet like-minded people online or in person!

Easy Rent
http://www.bnm.com

This user-friendly site lists over 100 rent-a-car agencies worldwide, all located near central airports. Book online and save yourself lots of hassle!

Nice Ride!
http://www.starwars.com/databank/star ship/millenniumfalcon/

Find out all about the ultimate dream machine – the Millennium Falcoln!

World of Classic Cars
http://www.classiccar.com

If you enjoy restoring old greats back to glory, you'll love this site. Everything you need to know about purchasing, restoring, and maintaining classic cars.

Smooth Ride
**http://www.jamesbondmm.co.uk/
vehicles.php**

Visit this site to find out about all the very special vehicles featured in classic Bond movies, like Goldfinger, Dr No, and You Only Live Twice.

211

Buick

http://www.buick-parts.com/carsbb.html

Great site for all Buick owners! Find the missing part you've been searching for, or discuss maintenance hiccups with your fellow Buick buddies.

Movie Mayhem

http://www.filmsite.org/moments_msc. html

Check out this site that documents the most impressive chase scenes from movies over the past hundred or so years.

Slot Cars
http://www.ncphobbies.com

If the only way you are going to be able to race a Formula One car is via the slot car track, then you'll be able to buy your slot cars here. Grown-ups only need apply!

The Automobile Homepage
http://www.auho.com

Whatever the make of car you're interested in, log on here for pictures, road test reports, and links to dealers.

213

Car Heaven
http://www.cars-on-line.com

This site is pure classic car heaven! All advertized classic cars on this site are shown with detailed info, so you will be able to purchase with confidence.

Get Kitted Out!
http://www.kitcar.com

A great site for kit car enthusiasts, featuring news, information on events, and even kit cars to buy!

Stick in the Mud
http://www.carstuck.com

If you've ever wanted to see a whole
bunch of vehicles stuck in the mud, then
this is the site for you. Photo galleries,
video clips, and much, much more.

Motional Memories
http://www.motionalmemories.com

If it's the image of classic cars that sets
your blood racing, this web site will take
it to boiling point! Superb photos of
super cars and vintage vehicles can be
found right here!

215

Sidecars
http://www.ural.com

The guys at this site import and distribute Russian Ural-style 1930s sidecar motorcycles worldwide – complete the online quiz to see if you deserve to become an owner of one of these classics.

Time Traveler?
**http://www.geocities.com/
MotorCity/Downs/7770**

Find out here all about the Delorean
sports car, the four-wheeled star of the
'Back to the Future' movies. Did you
know that only 6,500 were ever made?

Go!
http://www.formula1.com

There's some great information about
the Formula One teams at this site, and
also some slick links on who the drivers
are and who is currently in pole position.

Yahoo Cars
http://cars.yahoo.com

Before setting off to purchase your new car, check this online registry first. It lists all cars (both new and old) by make and model, and also has a research column.

Major or Minor
http://www.morrisminors.com

If you love vintage Morris Minors, here's a good place to discuss your passion! Don't delay – join the owner's club today!

The Door Fell Off!
http://www.carsurvey.org

A hilarious site full of disgruntled car owners detailing their motor problems. It's a good idea to log on here before spending your money to get the low-down on specific makes first!

Drive It Away
http://www.autotrader.com

Looking for a new or used car? Come here first. As well as reviews and specifications, they claim to have more than 1.5 million listings, updated daily!

Car City
http://www.carcity.com

Become a member at this site and they will provide a free 'reminder' service – you'll never forget to change the oil again!

Classic Directory
http://www.classic-car-directory.com

This hot wheel site has a search engine that links all the key components you need to purchase a classic car. Enter a search for the make you want and it will send dealer info back shortly after.

Old But Quick
http://www.bolide.co.uk

Bolide is an online magazine for classic car and historic motorsport enthusiasts. Bolide is actually a French expression meaning 'fast car'!

American Iron
http://www.americaniron.net

Visit this site to see hundreds of photos of classic American cars – and if you have one yourself, find out here how to repair and restore it. There's also a free online drag racing game!

221

F1 Live
http://www.f1-live.com

For all the Formula One action as it occurs, log on to this exhilarating site. It is overflowing with circuit information, vital statistics and facts about the daredevil drivers.

Drive Better
http://www.driving.co.uk

This comprehensive site has lots of hints and tips on how to be a better driver. It's UK-based, but much of the advice applies worldwide. Nice cartoons, too!

The Wheel Thing
http://www.sandsmachine.com
Buy a fold-up travel bike at this unusual
site and never worry about public
transport or parking spaces ever again!
It may also help to keep you fit and trim!

Auto Hit
http://www.team.net/www/museums/
If you are planning a world tour of
automotive museums you will find this
site invaluable! If not, it may just be
worth a look anyway.

223

Cool Biking
http://bicycling.about.com

What ever you want to know about cycling, you'll find it here – advice on maintenance and repair, safety, famous cyclists, cycle routes, and much more. A complete bikefest.

Environmental Issue
http://www.zapbikes.com

If it contains gas or diesel, this site won't sell it! But these guys do sell fantastic electric bikes, zappy scooters, and other modes of zero air pollution transport.

All About Cycles
http://www.cycletrader.com

Have a search through this web page before your settle on your next motor-cycle purchase. There are thousands of used and new motorcycles for sale, as well as links to other cool cycle sites.

Mega Bike
http://www.giant-bicycle.com

For all the latest racing news and the hottest bike info, log on to this giant of a site!

Big Dog Bikes
http://www.bigdogmotorcycles.com

'Big Dog' are the makers of distinctive American motorcycles – they make them to measure and no request is deemed too outlandish!

Harley Burly
http://www.legendmcs.com

If you don't want to part with your beloved Harley but it is in desperate need of parts, log on to this legendary motorcycle parts shop and keep your pride and joy up-to-scratch.

Ducati
http://www.ducati.com

Bid online at this Ducati Motor web site for memorabilia, or cruise through their virtual store that features bikes, clothing, and accessories. They also want to hear from you if you would like to open a Ducati store in your town!

Red Hot Honda
http://www.hondamotorcycles.com

This is the official Honda motorcycle web site, and it will give you the low-down on Honda's latest designs, specs and features. Plus there are details of their apprenticeship course!

101 For Sale
http://www.100motorcycles.com

Have your classified ad posted onto this web page, and it will automatically be sent to 100 others! Great place to look for a bike to purchase too!

Storm Chaser
http://www.stormeyes.org/tornado /vehicles/

An online tribute to the most bizarre vehicles that have been used as mobile scientific storm observation labs.

Yo Yamaha!
http://www.yamaha-motor.com

Check out the latest Yamaha bikes and accessories on this site, and get the latest news about their racing teams. Motocross, supercross, road racing, and more!

Kawasaki
http://www.kawasaki.com

View specs and photos of the bikes they produce, and read all the upcoming race information.

Talking Bikes
http://www.bikerheaven.com

Want advice on buying a bike, customizing it, tour planning, or even which biker gang to join? Log on here to chew the fat with fellow bikers from all over the world.

Motor World
http://www.motorworld.com
Imagine the leader of that biker gang you see cruising around! Now picture this online magazine in the same light! – hugely popular and packs a mean punch!

Come to Sid's!
http://www.mindspring.com/~bigsid
'Big Sid's' is a site for enthusiasts of fine motorcycles, both modern and classic. Read about Sid's latest restoration projects and his trips out on the road.

231

How Stuff Works
http://auto.howstuffworks.com/

Find out how car engines, brakes, tires, and even windshield wipers work with this factual and informative site.

Custom Chrome
http://www.customchrome.com/

links.phtml

A huge range of Harley-Davidson bike parts and accessories can be found here.

Hot Metal Mag
http://www.motorcycle.com

An online motorcycle magazine that features a monthly newsletter, a useful chat room, and practical road tests to make you king of the road.

Test Your Driving
http://www.worlddrivingschools.com/uk

If you are about to take the British driving test, why not do the theory exam in cyberspace first to check you are up to speed? You can take it several times if you wish!

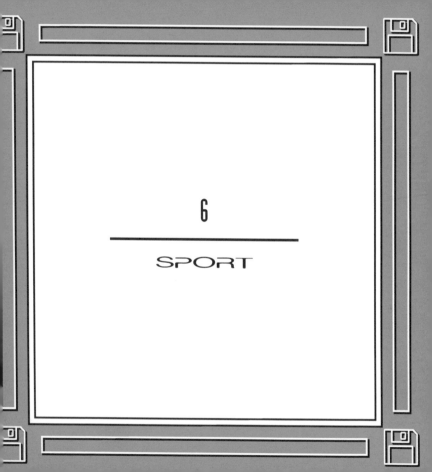

6

SPORT

Laptop Scores
http://sportsfeed.com

Missed another game because your girl-
friend wanted to watch 'Friends'? Have
your laptop close at hand and log on
here to read the scores as they come in.

Know It All!
http://www.allsports.com/

Perhaps the world's biggest and most
informative sports reference site,
featuring tons of information and gossip
on all sport around the globe.

Ultimate Hero
http://espn.go.com/sportscentury

Cool and comprehensive site dedicated to the sporting heroes of this century – find out who was the ultimate champion in each of your favorite sports.

To the Wall
http://www.allwall.com/asp/display-asp/_/ID--1834/1.asp

Vast megastore of sports' posters for wannabe quarterbacks. Have your favorite sports star sending out winning vibes from your bedroom wall!

Mini Sports Illustrated
http://www.sikids.com/index.html

All the info that the grown-up magazine contains (except for the babes in bikinis!), plus the added bonus of a computer games section.

Team Player
http://www.infobeat.com

Simply register your email address and Infobeat will inundate you with up-to-date info, such as scores and news on your favorite team.

237

Boxing Babes
http://www.insidewomensboxing.com

Get the lowdown on women's boxing
US style with 'Bad' Brad Berkwitt and his
colleagues. There are pics, fight reports,
and interviews with the leading
contenders. It's
sport, Jim, but not
as we know it.

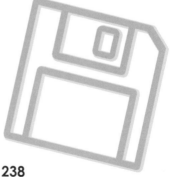

NFL
http://www.nfl.com

This is the official site of the National Football League, and it features a lot more than the non-official sites. Catch up on the locker room gossip and check out the scores!

All Sports
http://www.sports.com

If you're a sports fanatic, this is one site you must bookmark. It features up-to-date coverage of all the major sports from both sides of the Atlantic!

They Think It's All Over
http://www.soccerage.com

Fantastic video clips of some of the most famous goals in soccer. This site is enormous and features listings of teams worldwide.

Planet Rugby
http://www.planet-rugby.com

As the name suggests, this site is a winner in terms of worldwide rugby results, statistics, and players, so get down and dirty with your team.

Hockey Heaven
http://www.planetfieldhockey.com

If field hockey is your game, this site can't help but improve it. Every aspect of the game is covered, from world news through to in-depth practical advice for players and coaches.

Home Run
http://baseballguru.com/bbrings.html

Anything you want to know about America's favorite ball game, ask the 'Baseball Guru'! This massive site includes loads of information about the sport.

Speed!
http://www.daytonainternationalspeedway.com/

Strap on your seatbelt, adjust your helmet, and hold on tight! – this fantastic Daytona site is bang up-to-date with the latest, exhilarating racecar action.

Swedish Games
http://www.kfk.org

Join Sven and his friends as they battle the rest of the world for international Frisbee titles.

Dirtragmag
http://www.dirtragmag.com

Much more than the Tour de France, this terrific mountain bike ezine is packed to the brim with reviews, and health and fitness news, as well as an interactive opinion page.

Get the Rush!
http://www.aerial.org

Are you an adrenaline junkie? Then this site should give you a great fix of hair-raising action! You name it, these guys can organize for you to do it!

Table Tennis-tastic!
http://www.ittf.com

This site is a must for all fans of this amazingly fast-paced table game. It's packed with information, a chat room, and tips on how to beat the opponent!

Triathlon
http://www.triathletemag.com

Training schedules, diet tips and everything else in between can be found at this ezine site for greedy people not content with only doing one sport at a time!

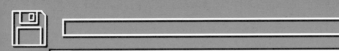

Hang Ten
http://www.surfermag.com/

Get away from your computer, slip into a wetsuit, and clear your mind. How? By surfing, of course! Read the low-down here before you hit the waves.

Ski Central
http://www.skicentral.com

Track down all the info you require to organize your winter sports program here. This site connects to over 5,500 snow sport sites and features ski reports and snow-cams.

Betting Bonanza
http://www.sporting-life.com

If you're thinking of placing a bet on an upcoming sport's event, check here for the insider tips first. Then check if you can afford to lose next week's rent money!

Cyberworkout
http://www.turnstep.com

No puffing and panting in an aerobics class any longer, because the future is cyber aerobics! Top instructors shriek encouragement to you all on one well-toned site!

Real Tennis
http://www.real-tennis.com/
history/main.html

'Real Tennis' started in Elizabethan England and was known as the 'Game of Kings'. Log on and check it out.

247

Howzat!
http://uk.cricinfo.com

Be bowled over by one of the best UK cricket sites around. News, reviews, and stats are all available on this site.

Scuba!
http://www.scubaduba.com

Dive into the web's ultimate scuba site. Amongst the raft of great features are interactive dive logs, photo galleries and exhibitions, and even a dive buddy directory!

Sporting Greats
http://www.foxsports.com/

For fans both young and old, there's loads here to amuse, inform and entertain on every sport imaginable.

Ice Cool!
http://www.fil-luge.org/index_en.htm

Get the lowdown here on the luge – probably the most dangerous of all winter sports. As well as competition news, you can find out how to get involved yourself (if you're mad enough!).

Golf Buggy
http://www.golfonline.com

Sit in your golf buggy and take in all the swinging action! All the results and play of the US Open, the PGA, the Masters, and the British Open, can be viewed here, and much more besides!

Sheer Height
http://www.bouldering.com

For lovers of risk and the great outdoors, this is the site for climbers who battle the rock-face in a game of strength, strategy, and cunning.

250

Americas Cup
http://www.americascup.com

The biggest boat race in the world!
This site captures the adrenaline and
windswept excitement as it happens!

Olympic Fever
http://www.olympic.org

What's great about this web site is that
you receive daily updates whilst the
Olympics are on, plus it's a brilliant
resource for the history of past Olympics
the remainder of the time!

251

Kicking Karate
http://www.martialinfo.com/

A fantastic site dedicated to martial arts. Find out here about the history, hall of fame, and current news. Here's where you learn the ultimate in focus, stamina and concentration.

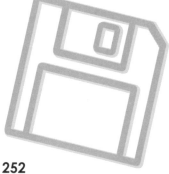

Karate Kids
http://www.martial-arts-network.com

Every kid wants to be either Bruce Lee
or the Karate Kid! Before you sign up for
a martial arts class, read this – it includes
a dictionary and info on how to start.

Sport Drug
**http://fullcoverage.yahoo.com/
full_coverage/sports/drugs_in_sports**

Whether it's a news-breaking scandal at
the Olympics, or the test results of a diet
supplement, you'll find the coverage
and results at this fascinating site.

Raging Bull
http://www.boxing-central.com/

Not a site for the faint-hearted, this boxing site has all the latest macho action including news, schedules, and results.

Marathon Man
http://www.runnersworld.com

This track and athletics site features a time calculator, which may prove useful to plan how long it will take you to dash down to the bar before closing!

Checkmate!
http://www.chess.net

You can play online either socially or competitively, plus find information on events and tournaments and all the news from the world of chess.

Ice Magic
http://www.aggressive.com

Excellent site for skating fans. Post your message on the bulletin board and share tips and gossip with other speed freaks.

Riding High
http://www.mountainzone.com

A site dedicated to mountain sports: snowboarding, mountain biking, hiking, skiing and climbing. Read about, and see photos of, the exploits of others here, then start planning your own expedition!

Winter Olympics
http://www.winterolympics.com

Current and past information mix online at the coolest winter sports site. Get in touch with your inner snowman!

Golf Universe
http://www.playgolfnow.com

Think of this great site as the golfing
bible – all you and your tee need to
know before heading outside onto the
fairways.

Basket Case
**http://www.geocities.com/
colosseum/court/3753/index.html**

Want to improve your basketball
technique? Check out Coach Rowe's
hints and tips at this cool site!

Sports Halls
http://www.sportshalls.com/search.cfm

Every sport, in every country around the globe has a 'Hall of Fame' tucked away somewhere – and this site is where they all meet!

Putter Along
http://www.cybergolf.com

Cybergolf claims to be THE source for local golf knowledge. Find your nearest course, then print off free discount coupons you can use there!

High as a Kite!
http://www.kitesurfing.org/

Imagine being pulled across the water by a big kite whilst balancing on a surfboard or wakeboard. Imagine no longer! Everything you want to know about this exciting sport – pictures and words – can be found here at the official site of the UK Kitesurfing Organization!

Big League
http://www.eteamz.com/baseball/instruction/tips

Log in here for tips on being a better baseball player. All aspects of the sport are covered, from pitching to base-running. There's also a coaches' corner with advice and drills.

NHL
http://www.nhl.com

The official National Hockey League web site, where there is plenty of action and bruised shins to be viewed!

Judo Masters
http://judoinfo.com

This site claims to be the world's biggest virtual judo club, with comprehensive information about the sport and art of judo.

U Bet!
http://www.sportingbet.com

If you fancy a spot of cockroach racing, this site will lead you to the action, otherwise you can also check out form, hot tips, and all the info you need about online betting.

Fun Fractions
http://www.tsoft.com/~deano

Make fractions more fun! This homework site sets out to prove that, together, math and science can be applied to basketball!

NBA
http://www.nba.com

The official site of the National Basketball Association. All the player profiles, past and present scores, and dream memorabilia for the avid collector, can be found here.

Hitting Trees
http://www.skinet.com

Log on to this site for step-by-step instructions on learning to ski. You'll probably fall over, but at least you'll do it like a pro!

Go to the Max
http://www.allextremesports.com/

Extreme, out-of-control sports for you to dream about are featured here. If you want to make the dream a reality, pull the cord…if you dare!

Fat Tyre
http://www.mbronline.com

Resource site for mountain biking
junkies. A brilliant source for facts about
mountain biking destinations, upcoming
challenges, and trail information.

Ezine Ball Boy
http://www.tennis.com

Get the advantage at this regularly
updated online magazine that details
upcoming matches, tips from those in
the know, and hot player profiles.

Reservoir Dogs
http://www.discdog.com

This cool canine site will give you hot tips on training your pooch to go one better than 'Go, fetch', and actually catch a Frisbee in its mouth! Hours of fun for you both!

Back at You!
http://www.tennisserver.com

An interactive tennis site that serves up the questions and then volleys them straight at you!

Wipe Out!
http://www.surfermag.com

The best way to get wiped out is by a wave crashing over your head whilst experiencing the exhilarating sport of surfing. This fantastic site outlines upcoming surf events and tips for beginners.

What's Curling?
http://www.brown.edu/ Students/Brown_Curling_Club/ info/expl.html

This is an excellent introduction to the sport. The site includes diagrams and cool video clips.

Couch Potato Star
http://www.sports-gaming.com

Stay home, drink beer, play tons of brilliant games, and become a hero without the inconvenience of having to get out of your comfy chair!

Euro Hockey
http://www.eurohockey.net

Find news on every European professional hockey team – and it's all written in English so you'll have no trouble with translation!

Switch Skateboarding
http://www.switchmagazine.com

Swing by the site of this cool skateboarding magazine. It has video clips and photo galleries, plus step-by-step advice on performing tricks such as kickflips to fakie and backside lipslides!

Strike One!
http://www.beabetterhitter.com

Every aspect of baseball is covered here, with online video clips to illustrate the points made. Check out the 'Baseball Bloopers' page for some light relief!

Big Bowl
http://www.superbowl.com

Companies don't pay eye-watering rates to place their advert near this game for nothing! Log on to the 'Superbowl' site to find out why.

Your Old Kitbag
http://www.kitbag.com

Do you want to be Number Eight in your favorite team? Here you can buy yourself the team colors and view the latest uniforms for the season.

Cybercycling
http://www.cyclery.com

Here's a top site for cyclists, with forums, discussion lists, and free email newsletters on all things bicycle related. There's even a job board for those who dream of working in a cycle shop...

Manage Your Own Soccer Team
http://www.fantasyfootball.telegraph.co.uk/

One of the best fantasy football sites around – choose your ideal blend of English or European soccer stars online and, for a small price, you can manage your very own 'dream team'!

Block It!
http://www.volleyball.org

If volleyball is your game, this is the site for you. Everything is covered about the sport with loads of links too!

271

FA Premiership
http://www.thefa.com

The official soccer FA site with tons of links, backgrounds on your favorite soccer stars, and tips from the best players in the business.

Howzat!
http://www.cricinfo.com

Cricinfo describes itself as the home of cricket on the Internet, and with news, feature articles, live test match scores, and detailed stats on players around the world it's hard to argue with that!

Davis Cup
http://www.daviscup.org
Up-to-the-minute site on the annual
Britain versus America, Davis Cup tennis
matches. It also includes an interesting
reference section about the game and
its stars.

Scrum
http://www.scrum.com

This site was voted one of the best rugby information sites on the Web. Check out the famous quotes from the greatest of players!

Football with Attitude
http://www.gridirongrumblings.com

Here you'll find National Football League news and rumors, and player and team statistics. There are also message boards where you can swap NFL gossip with other fans.

274

Icy Action
http://www.wintersport.as

Get the latest winter sports news at this
site, which specializes in biathlon, ski
jumping, Nordic combined and cross-
country. Cool in every sense!

Run the World!
http://www.runtheplanet.com

If you're a keen runner and enjoy
traveling, check out this site, which
will tell you the best places to go
running anywhere in the world, as
recommended by the locals.

275

Box Seats
http://boxing.about.com

'Float like a butterfly, sting like a bee'
at this site, which contains news, articles,
world rankings, and links to a wide
range of other boxing web pages.

Snowboarders
http://www.skicentral.com

Uncertain about where to take your
board next snowboarding season?
Whizz off in the right direction at this
great web site that has an index of the
best snow sites each season.

Get Blown Away
http://www.windsports.net

At this site you can learn all about winter wind sports, including ice sailing, kite surfing, skate sailing, ice boating, and ice surfing. Wrap up warm though!

It's Snow Joke
http://cnn.com/travel/ski.report

On your next ski vacation, you'll be wanting to know what the snow coverage is like that day – this site has a direct link to CNN that will instantly answer the question.

US Lacrosse
http://www.lacrosse.org/

Log on here for articles, news stories, and photo galleries devoted to this fast-moving sport.

Making a Racket
http://www.tennisone.com

Whether you enjoy singles, doubles, mixed doubles, or just restringing your racket, this site is a one-stop tennis bonanza.

Row Your Boat
http://users.ox.ac.uk/~quarrell/

This excellent web site is home to 'The Rowing Service', which will happily connect you to thousands of rowing links worldwide.

I'll Take Two
http://www.2-tickets.com

Click on to find very cheap tickets to worldwide sporting events, such as Formula One, NFL games and boxing matches.

280

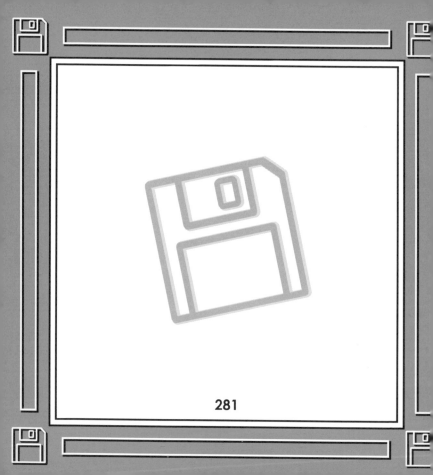

281

OTHER TITLES IN THE SERIES:

500 of the World's Best Web Sites
ISBN: 1-902813-30-8

500 of the Weirdest and Wackiest Web Sites
ISBN: 1-902813-29-4

282

LAGOON
BOOKS